SPORTS GREAT JOE MONTANA

—Sports Great Books—

Sports Great Jim Abbott (ISBN 0-89490-395-0)

Sports Great Charles Barkley (ISBN 0-89490-386-1)

Sports Great Larry Bird (ISBN 0-89490-368-3)

Sports Great Bobby Bonilla (ISBN 0-89490-417-5)

Sports Great Will Clark (ISBN 0-89490-390-X)

Sports Great Roger Clemens (ISBN 0-89490-284-9)

Sports Great John Elway (ISBN 0-89490-282-2)

Sports Great Patrick Ewing (ISBN 0-89490-369-1)

Sports Great Orel Hershiser (ISBN 0-89490-389-6)

Sports Great Bo Jackson (ISBN 0-89490-281-4)

Sports Great Magic Johnson (Revised and Expanded) (ISBN 0-89490-348-9)

Sports Great Michael Jordan (ISBN 0-89490-370-5)

Sports Great Kevin Mitchell (ISBN 0-89490-388-8)

Sports Great Joe Montana (ISBN 0-89490-371-3)

Sports Great Hakeem Olajuwon (ISBN 0-89490-372-1)

Sports Great Kirby Puckett (ISBN 0-89490-392-6)

Sports Great Jerry Rice (ISBN 0-89490-419-1)

Sports Great Cal Ripken (ISBN 0-89490-387-X)

Sports Great David Robinson (ISBN 0-89490-373-X)

Sports Great Nolan Ryan (ISBN 0-89490-394-2)

Sports Great Barry Sanders (ISBN 0-89490-418-3)

Sports Great Darryl Strawberry (ISBN 0-89490-291-1)

Sports Great Isiah Thomas (ISBN 0-89490-374-8)

Sports Great Herschel Walker (ISBN 0-89490-207-5)

SPORTS GREAT JOE MONTANA

Jack Kavanagh

—*Sports Great Books*—

ENSLOW PUBLISHERS, INC.
44 Fadem Road   P.O. Box 38
Box 699   Aldershot
Springfield, N.J. 07081   Hants GU12 6BP
U.S.A.   U.K.

Copyright ©1992 by Jack Kavanagh

All rights reserved.

No part of this book may be reproduced by any means without the written permission of the publisher.

Library of Congress Cataloging-in-Publication Data

Kavanagh, Jack
    Sports great Joe Montana / Jack Kavanagh.
      p. cm. — (Sports great books)
    Includes index.
    Summary: Follows the life of the San Francisco 49ers quarterback, from his childhood to the present.
    ISBN 0-89490-371-3
    1. Montana, Joe, 1956– —Juvenile literature. 2. Football players—United States—Biography—Juvenile literature. 3. San Francisco 49ers (Football team)—Juvenile literature. [1. Montana, Joe, 1956– . 2. Football players.] I. Title. II. Series.
GV939.M59K38
796.332'092—dc20
[B]
                                                        91- 41527
                                                            CIP
                                                             AC

Printed in the United States of America

10 9 8 7 6

Photo Credits: Robert F. Lindquist, pp. 8, 19, 20, 25, 27, 29, 36, 38, 39, 40, 44, 46, 48, 50, 53, 55, 57, 59; University of Notre Dame Sports Information Department, pp. 11, 14.

Cover Photo: Robert F. Lindquist

Contents

Chapter 1 7

Chapter 2 17

Chapter 3 23

Chapter 4 33

Chapter 5 43

Chapter 6 52

    Career Statistics 62

    Index 63

Chapter 1

Joe Montana is a winner. Quarterbacks are measured in a lot of ways. The record books tell us how many passes they threw, how many were caught, how many went for touchdowns, and how many were intercepted. Statistics give us the yards gained in each game, in each season, and, at the end of the player's career, his lifetime totals.

Joe Montana measures up to the best, but there is one special talent that is very much his own. No field leader has ever brought his team from behind to victory more often than Joe. He just won't give up, and he won't let his team quit while there is a tick left on the clock.

Football fans first noticed Joe Montana's come-from-behind heroics when he was in college. If it had happened once or twice, those games might be remembered as special occasions. But it soon became almost mystical the way Notre Dame would pull out tough games that seemed lost as Montana's passes and scrambling runs turned the tide at the finish.

Freshmen did not play on the varsity team when Joe

Montana arrived at South Bend, Indiana. He had to wait until his sophomore year before he played his way into the lineup. As a matter of fact, he had to wait until the third game of the season. Notre Dame was five deep in quarterbacks, and the new coach, Dan Devine, could not seem to make up his mind about any of them.

Finally, when the older quarterbacks could not move the team against an underdog Northwestern University, the coach sent Joe Montana into the game. Bang, bang, and bang! Notre Dame tied the score, 7–7, on a drive with halfback Al Hunter crashing over from the 2-yard line. A few plays later it was fullback Jim Browner plowing 12 yards on a pitchout from Montana. Next Notre Dame scored on Montana's first touchdown toss, 14 yards down the middle to Mark McLane. The Fighting Irish kept on scoring, with Joe Montana adding the final touchdown himself, faking a pitch and running in from the 6-yard line for a 31–7 victory.

Cheer, cheer for old Notre Dame? Hardly. Northwestern was a soft touch on the schedule, and Montana had simply called the right plays. It was the debut of a player who would become a great star, but it did not even win him a starting role. The next week Joe Montana sat on the bench until the fourth quarter against the very tough University of North Carolina. Notre Dame was trailing 14–6 and was back on its own 27-yard line before Coach Dan Devine finally turned the game over to Joe.

Then, in five plays, two of them on-the-button passes, Al Hunter crashed in to make it 14–12. Notre Dame elected to try a two-point conversion, and Joe hit Doug Buth to tie the score.

North Carolina worked the ball close enough to try a 26-yard field goal and missed. It was Notre Dame's ball with 1:15 left. That was enough for Joe Montana. The first play from the Irish 20-yard line went nowhere. There was now 1:03

left on the clock. Coach Devine called for a draw play, but Joe Montana saw that the Carolina cornerback, Russ Conley, was playing deep. Joe changed the play, calling for a pass with an audible. He hit Ted Burgmeier on the sideline. When Conley tried to intercept the pass, he slipped, and Burgmeier scampered 80 yards for the game-winning touchdown. The pattern had been set for Joe Montana. Before the season ended, he wrote another storybook finish, this time against the Air Force Academy. With Notre Dame trailing 30–10 and only ten minutes to play, he brought the team back for a 31–30 victory.

Then Montana's career was put on hold for a whole season. The next fall his collar bone was broken in a preseason scrimmage, and he sat out the year. In one way, it worked to his advantage. During his sophomore year he had been on academic probation. Notre Dame asks more of its athletes than ability on the playing field. It expects them to be full-time students and to earn a degree. Joe studied accounting, far from a snap course. He also had an added distraction. During his freshman year, Joe and Kim Moses, his hometown sweetheart, impulsively got married. The year he did not play football, he hit the books hard. He also used the extra year of varsity eligibility his injury gave him to stay in school an extra semester. He would be a December graduate. The additional months would give him more time to get ready for a professional career.

It was during his final two seasons at Notre Dame that Joe Montana developed into a national figure. In 1977, after a season away from the field, he had to start out again as the third-string quarterback. He did not get a chance until the third game of the season and not until his team was trailing Purdue 24–14 with two minutes left in the third quarter. A field goal brought the Irish within a touchdown of the Boilermakers.

Then the "Montana magic" went to work. He hit tight end Ken MacAfee with a 13-yard scoring pass, and the game was tied. With time running out, Joe hit on two long passes to set up the winning touchdown. David Mitchell ran the ball in with only 1:39 left to play. Montana had completed 9 of 14 passes for a 31–24 victory. Back as the starting quarterback, Joe led Notre Dame to a national championship. However, it took a post-season win, 38–10 over the nationally Number-One-ranked University of Texas in the Cotton Bowl, to prove Notre Dame was really the top team.

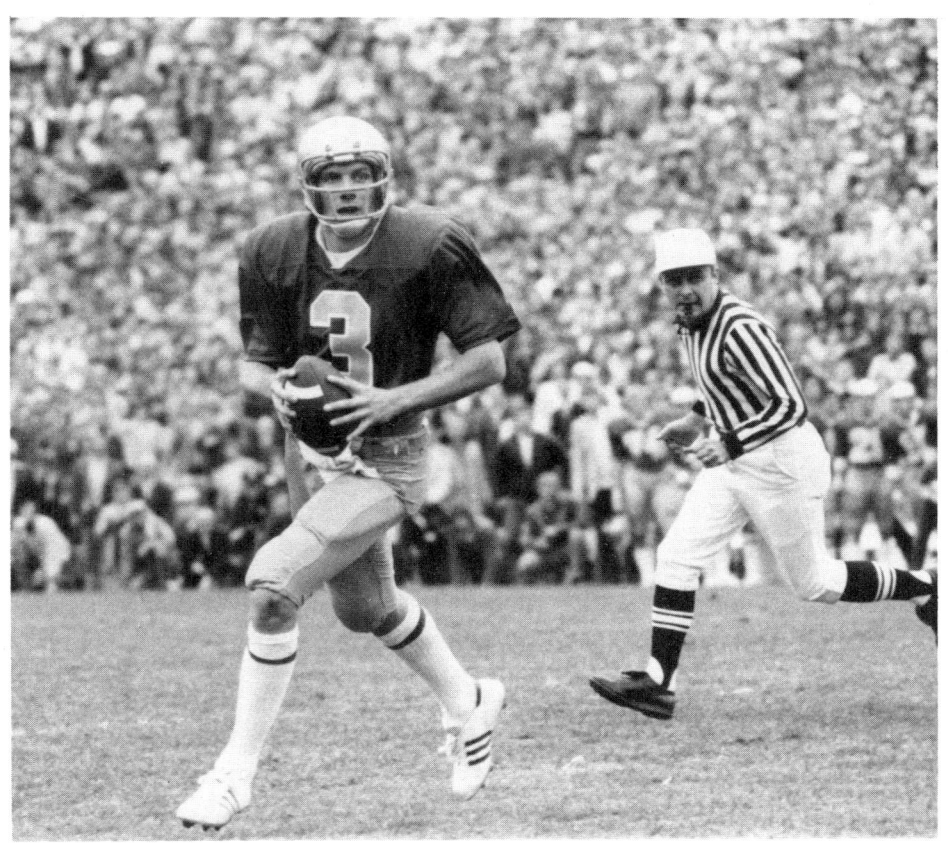

Joe Montana scrambling at Notre Dame.

The 1978 Cotton Bowl was played in Dallas, home of the Texas Longhorns. With the Heisman Trophy winner, Earl Campbell, and the Outland Trophy winner, Brad Shearer, on their team Texas was favored to win. Instead, Notre Dame swamped them! It wasn't even close. Joe Montana hardly had to throw the ball. The backs, Jerome Heavens and Vegas Ferguson, each ran for more than 100 yards. The Notre Dame defense shut down Campbell and held Texas scoreless through the second half for a 38–10 victory. Notre Dame replaced Texas in the polls as the Number One team.

Joe Montana's final season at Notre Dame produced a 9–3 record with still more of those come-from-behind games people now expected from him. With Notre Dame trailing Pittsburgh 17–7 with eight minutes left, Montana completed 15 passes for 218 yards and a 26–17 victory. The Fighting Irish pulled one out of the fire from Tennessee and almost did it with an unbelievable comeback against Southern California. Late in the fourth quarter, Joe drove his team from three touchdowns behind to take the lead. Then the fates that had always smiled on him turned fickle. The Trojans edged to victory with a field goal in the last second. However, the Fighting Irish were invited back to the Cotton Bowl for what would be Joe Montana's final college game.

The 1979 Cotton Bowl was played under terrible conditions, and Joe Montana was a very sick man. He had come down with a flu bug and had gone to bed early at the team's hotel. When he looked out the window in the morning, he rubbed his runny eyes. Ice! As a boy in western Pennsylvania, ice had meant you could skate on the nearby pond. But, Texas? The state he had always thought of as part of "the sunny South" was glazed with frozen crystal. In addition, a wind chill factor made it feel like it was ten degrees. The frigid wind whistled through a partially filled stadium. Almost 40,000 ticket holders decided to stay home and watch the game on television. The maintenance crew at the Cotton Bowl shoveled inch-thick ice off the field. Notre Dame won the toss and, with a thirty-mile-an-hour-wind behind them, quickly went ahead, 12–0. Then it was Houston's turn, and they literally breezed to a 20–12 lead. All the scoring was done at the sheltered end of the stadium, where the wind was not blowing at gale force.

A very ill Joe Montana dragged himself to the locker room at halftime. Not only was he weakened by flu and numb, frozen fingers, but his body temperature had dropped to an alarming 96 degrees. Joe shook uncontrollably. He was wrapped in blankets, and hot chicken soup was poured into him. Gradually he stopped shaking, but another quarterback, Tim Koegel, took over. The game continued to slip away, and with less than five minutes remaining in the third quarter, Notre Dame was behind, 34–12. On the sidelines, Joe Montana blew on his hands. He wanted to get back into the game. When he did return, he threw an interception, his third of the day. Then the fourth quarter began. Time for the "Comeback Kid" to go to work. The wind was now behind the Fighting Irish, and Montana used it. After an intercepted pass gave Notre Dame a quick touchdown, Montana passed to Vegas Ferguson for a two-point conversion. The score had closed to 34–20.

When Notre Dame held Houston and took over on its own 39-yard line, Joe Montana had 5:40 left to overcome a two-touchdown lead. His passes moved the team closer, and an interference call against the Cougars put the ball on the 3-yard line. Joe ran the ball in on the third play. Then he added two points with a pass to Kris Haines. Notre Dame now trailed, 34–28.

Again the Irish defense held Houston and gave Montana

the ball at midfield with 2:25 left in the game. But before Joe could rescue another game, he lost the ball on a fumble. Houston defensive back David Hodge ripped the ball out of Montana's chilled hands after he had run 20 yards and Houston had the ball with 2:05 left. Once again the defensive team held the Cougars. They had to kick into the gale-force wind from their own 24-yard line with 46 seconds left. It was only a short punt, but Notre Dame had been offside. Now, needing only one yard for a first down, Houston went for it. They did not make it! It was Notre Dame's ball with 28 seconds to play and 29 yards to go. A field goal would not do it. Notre Dame needed a touchdown to win.

Joe fooled everyone by running for 11 yards. Next he hit on a short pass to Kris Haines on the 8-yard line. Joe's next

Joe Montana in formation at Notre Dame.

throw was again to Haines, but he missed a wide-open target. The clock was stopped with two seconds left.

Coach Dan Devine and Joe met for a conference at the sideline. Asked what play he wanted to call, Montana convinced the coach they should re-run the play that had just missed. This time it worked. Kris Haines dove, caught the ball inches above the ground, and skidded across the icy field with the ball tightly held in his grip. The score was tied. Fate was still teasing Notre Dame. When Joe Unis, who had grown up in Dallas, kicked the conversion, an illegal procedure call against the Irish nullified the play. Calmly, he did it again, and the game ended 35–34.

This was Joe Montana's farewell to college football. His career at Notre Dame ended as it began, with Joe driving his team to another come-from-behind victory. His career with the Fighting Irish had been shortened by injuries, but even so, he had completed 268 passes out of 515 attempts and scored 25 touchdowns. That so many of them came when his team was behind and brought the team to victory was Joe Montana's special contribution to the history of Notre Dame football. Next he would try the professional game.

Chapter 2

When he graduated from Notre Dame, Joe Montana headed west. After freezing to death in the Cotton Bowl, he wanted the warmth of southern California. If the folks back in Monongahela, Pennsylvania, had expected him to return home, they were disappointed. Like other great quarterbacks who had come from the gritty towns in the western end of the state, he would find an NFL city and make it his. Broadway Joe Namath had claimed New York, and Johnny Unitas was Mr. Baltimore Football for over a decade. George Blanda had passed and kicked field goals in Chicago, and Montana's contemporary rival, Dan Marino, would stake out Florida with Miami. Jim Kelly would make Buffalo his home turf. Joe Montana did not know his future would be with the San Francisco 49ers. He just made a beeline for the West Coast and waited until he was picked up in the NFL draft.

Actually, despite his national acclaim for comeback victories at Notre Dame, Joe was not rated as a great prospect for the pros. Even though he is listed at 6 feet, 2 inches and 195 pounds, he is a spindly legged, narrow-shouldered man.

He also had a reputation for getting hurt. The teams in professional football are bigger than those he faced in college and were looking for tall, rangy quarterbacks who could throw over the outstretched arms of rushing linemen. Big men, like Terry Bradshaw of the Pittsburgh Steelers, had set the standard in the late 1970s. It did not seem likely that Joe Montana, the nimble-footed newcomer would develop into the "Passer of the Eighties." Yet, even though the 49ers waited until the third round to select him, it was his quickness that had caught the eye of the new San Francisco head coach, Bill Walsh.

Walsh was the right coach for Joe Montana, and the recruit was ideal for Bill Walsh's style of play. After ten seasons as an assistant coach in the NFL, Bill Walsh had been named general manager and head coach of the tail-end San Francisco 49ers. The team needed to be rebuilt, and Joe Montana had just the right abilities to make it a winner—maybe even a champion.

Quarterbacks hardly ever become starters in their first professional season. It takes a year or two to learn the ropes. There was no pressure on Montana to win at once. In fact, he only backed up the holdover quarterback, Steve DeBerg. His main role was to spot the ball for placekicker Ray Wersching on extra points and field goal tries. Since the team won only two games during Joe's first year, he was not called on to hold the ball for conversions very often.

The 49ers brought Joe Montana along very carefully. To build up his confidence, he was never thrown into a hopelessly lost game. Instead, he would take over when the ball was in good field position. If San Francisco had a good chance to score, they would try to have Joe Montana lead the drive.

The 1979 season was all but written off. The great super running back, O. J. Simpson, played his farewell season for the 49ers. He had slowed down and was often hurt. However, he served as an inspiration to Joe and made him feel welcome among the professionals. Joe also teamed up with another rookie who was to become his favorite pass receiver. Dwight Clark and Joe Montana had played against each other in college. Clark had been a whiz at catching passes for Clemson University, and now he would be on the receiving end of those thrown by Montana.

Coach Walsh saw he had a natural passing combination in Montana and Clark and let the two rookies work together. Mostly, Joe Montana concentrated on learning Walsh's system. It was much different from what had been used at Notre Dame. In college Joe had called signals that told the receivers what routes to run. In the pros, the numbers he called told the other backs who was to block. Receivers ran routes that seemed to offer the best opportunity to get open. Joe had

Montana talking over a play with San Francisco coach Bill Walsh.

to become familiar with what they did so he would know where they would be when he threw the ball.

Joe Montana's first year with the San Francisco 49ers was a learning experience. The team repeated its poor showing of the year before, again ending with a 2–14 record. Joe made brief appearances in 16 games, completing 13 of the 23 passes he threw, one for a touchdown.

The next year started the same way. Steve DeBerg was the quarterback, but Coach Walsh was getting ready to put Joe Montana in charge. After DeBerg had seven passes intercepted against Dallas in the sixth game of the season, Walsh began to

Joe gets ready to pass to an open receiver.

use Joe a lot more. Dwight Clark became his first choice as a receiver, and the team began to improve.

Although he was playing cautiously, still learning the defenses against which he had to pass, Joe led the NFL in passing percentage. He completed 176 of 273 passes for a 64.5 percentage. He threw for two touchdowns. More importantly, to show what the future held for his team, Joe pulled off his first come-from-behind win.

After a lackluster first half against the New Orleans Saints on December 7, 1980, San Francisco trailed by 28 points. In the second half, Joe led the 49ers in four touchdown drives, two on his passes and two on runs. The game went into overtime, and Joe Montana guided his team on a 55-yard drive that set up a field goal to win the game. It showed the San Francisco fans that Joe Montana was the same "Comeback Kid" he had been at Notre Dame. The team's record improved to 6–10. The 1980s had begun, and San Francisco was about to become the dominant team of the decade. Joe Montana was ready to claim the title as the best quarterback of the 1980s.

Chapter 3

Coach Bill Walsh named Joe Montana the starting quarterback in 1981. Steve DeBerg was traded to the Denver Broncos, and the job of leading the San Francisco 49ers belonged to Joe. He was more relaxed, more confident. He knew that his offensive linemen would set up a strong pocket to protect him. The key to winning in the NFL is to have a dominant offensive line. The five men who formed this unit for the 49ers were John Ayers, Randy Cross, Keith Fahnhorst, Fred Quillan, and Dan Audick. They became a tightly knit unit, helping each other keep Joe from being sacked until he could find an open man. Joe's best friend on the team, Dwight Clark, most often would be his target. Not that Joe was playing favorites, but the rangy receiver always seemed to get open in clutch situations.

The team's defensive backfield was another part of the team that suddenly jelled. The leader was Dwight Hicks, who had come to the team with Montana in the '79 college draft. The others who became known as "Dwight Hicks and the Hot Licks" had all come from the '81 draft. The most ferocious of them was Ronnie Lott from USC. He was the hit man, after knocking the ball loose with jarring tackles.

Even though the team had improved, the 49ers lost their first two games. Then came a decisive win over Dallas, 45–10, and soon San Francisco began to climb in the standings of the NFC Western Division. They were the first team to clinch a division title that year and were the first San Francisco team to reach the playoffs in nine years. The 49ers won 13 games, the most the team had ever won. Again Joe Montana's pass completion percentage was the highest in the NFL. He completed 311 of 488 attempts for 3,565 yards and 19 touchdowns. He had the lowest interception rate in his division, second best in the whole NFL.

After they had beaten the New York Giants, 38–17, in the NFC's semifinal game, the 49ers had to play Dallas. San Francisco would have the home-field advantage and play the game in Candlestick Park. However, the Cowboys had crushed Tampa Bay in the other semifinal and were out to avenge the regular season game they had lost to San Francisco back in October.

The 49ers team was weakened by a flu bug, and Dallas outplayed them for three quarters. Joe was having an off day, with three of his passes intercepted. In all, San Francisco had six turnovers, two leading to Dallas touchdowns. They also drew critical penalty calls from the officials that led to 10 more Dallas points.

With 4:54 left on the clock, the 49ers were behind 27–21. They were deep in their own end of the field, on the 11-yard line. There was time for one final drive. Some teams might have tried to hit on long passes, but Joe Montana is a wizard at moving the team in short bursts. His sideline passes stop the clock as he comes closer and closer to the enemy's goal line. Joe mixed in short gainers and runs as the 49ers zigzagged

With no open receiver, Montana runs with the ball to add some extra yardage.

their way up the field. They reached the Dallas 6-yard line with just under a minute left to play. It was third down when the Cowboys called time out.

This gave Joe a chance to trot over to the sideline and calmly review the options with Coach Walsh. It would be the biggest decision of the season. Call the right play and they would be headed for the Super Bowl. Pick the wrong one and their season was over. Joe is a good runner in the clutch, so the coach called an option play. Joe would sprint to his right and look for a receiver. Only if he could not spot anyone breaking clear would he try to slip past the rugged Dallas defense.

Joe's first target would be the wide receiver, Freddie Solomon. If Freddie was covered, the next choice would be Dwight Clark. If no one was open, Joe could run or throw the ball out of bounds. There would still be one last down left. The ball was snapped to Joe, and the huge Dallas line charged. Ed "Too Tall" Jones (6 feet, 9 inches) led the way, and Joe saw that Freddie was covered. He kept running to his right, looking for Clark. Actually, Joe did not see his favorite target break into the clear. By now he instinctively knew where he would be. Joe pump-faked once and then let the ball go on a high, hard throw. If Dwight Clark could not get up far enough to catch it, then the ball would be too high to be intercepted. Dwight leaped higher than anyone thought he could jump and caught the ball on his fingertips. Joe, flattened by the Dallas defenders, knew from the crowd that Clark had come down with the ball and tied the score. When Ray Wersching kicked the extra point, San Francisco went ahead 28–27. Dallas had one last turn, but their quarterback, Danny White, fumbled, and San Francisco end Jim Stuckey fell on the ball. The 49ers were on their way to Super Bowl XVI.

These championship games are identified by Roman numerals to make it easier to relate them to their

Joe celebrates a successful touchdown pass.

championship seasons. The NFL season ends in December. The Super Bowl is played in January of the next year. When the two 1981 conference winners of the NFL met to decide the championship, the game was actually played in 1982.

The Super Bowl takes place on a neutral field so no one has a home-crowd advantage. It is also played where the weather is not expected to be a factor. On January 24, 1982, the championship game was played in the Silverdome, an almost fully enclosed stadium in Pontiac, Michigan. The 1981 season had opened there for the 49ers, and they had been beaten by the Detroit Lions. They had come a long way since then and did not think the field would be a jinx.

San Francisco, winner of the National Football Conference, met the Cincinnati Bengals, who had finished on top in the American Football Conference. They were led by another quarterback who had been developed by Bill Walsh, Kenny Anderson.

For once San Francisco did not have to ask Joe Montana to pull the game out of the fire. In fact, they almost let it slip away. Joe had scored one touchdown and passed for another early in the game. With a pair of Ray Wersching field goals added in, the 49ers were ahead 20–0 at halftime.

The Bengals came back strong in the second half, and only a stiff goal line stand in the third quarter slowed Cincinnati's surge. The 49ers hung on and became Super Bowl champions, 26–21. Joe completed 14 of 22 passes for 157 yards and was named the game's Most Valuable Player. It was an honor Joe Montana accepted with his usual modesty. He regretted that it did not include the kicking contributions of Ray Wersching and the strong San Francisco defense. However, Ross Browner, a stalwart of Cincinnati's defense, thought his former teammate at Notre Dame deserved the MVP award.

"Joe played a fine game," the rugged defensive end told

An anxious Montana hoping to hold onto San Francisco's lead.

reporters. "This was a game that showcased his talent." Browner explained that Montana had never really been appreciated by Dan Devine, the Notre Dame coach. "Joe was just too cool, too calm and collected."

Jim Plunkett, the former star quarterback of the Oakland Raiders, talked about Montana's "intangibles," which he said are what make a good quarterback. "Scrambling to get out of trouble, coming up with the big play when you need it—those are things you can't draw on chalkboards."

Praise like this, coming from other players, meant more to Joe Montana than all the headlines and columns written about him. The only problem he now had was to stay on top of the pinnacle he had reached in only his first year as the San Francisco 49ers' starting quarterback. The next year, 1982, the whole league slid downhill.

The 49ers lost their first two games, and then the National Football League Players Association went on strike for seven weeks. Joe Montana does not belong to the union. He insisted he would have joined in the protest had the union's goals been the right ones. Joe believed the real issue was "free agency." The major league baseball players get extraordinary salaries by being able to change teams when their individual contracts end. Instead, the NFL Players Association had its eyes on directly sharing in the money the team owners took in, particularly from television rights.

Joe and many other players said the union had the horse behind the cart. They were pushing when they should be pulling together to get the same kind of deal big league baseball players enjoyed. If the player can negotiate a new contract when the old one ends, the owners will bid against each other. That is how salaries are increased, Montana argued. The team was divided, and the owners stood together. By the time the fifty-seven-day-long strike was settled, almost half the season had been wasted. Even worse, the 49ers, the Super Bowl Champions, were torn apart by the disagreements among players. They lost six of the nine games that were left on the schedule. Joe's stats were impressive. He completed 213 of 346 passes for 61.5 percent. His 17 touchdowns were far greater than the 11 interceptions made against him. A good way to show that one is a successful passer is to have more touchdowns than interceptions. Despite his own stats, the 1982 season was one Joe Montana would rather forget.

Chapter 4

The bitter 1982 season also ended Joe Montana's original four-year $500,000 a season contract. It had been a lot of money when it was signed, but players were getting far more after the strike was over. People filled the stadiums for NFL games, no matter how much the tickets cost. They paid to park their cars. They bought programs, hot dogs, and souvenirs. Money flowed in during the 1980s, and the TV networks bid up the cost to televise the games. Joe Montana's agent, Larry Monroe, went after a new three-year deal that would pay at least a million and a half dollars. The young man from the blue-collar community of Monongahela, Pennsylvania, could afford an expensive lifestyle. However, money did not change his values.

Joe, an only child, had been deeply involved with sports since he was a little boy. His father, Joseph Montana, Sr., was the manager of a finance company. His mother was a secretary for the company. Mr. Montana was a topnotch local athlete, and he encouraged his son to take up sports. There was a basketball hoop in the backyard and a tire swinging on a rope so Joe could practice passing a football accurately. In the winter, basketball filled the bill. Joe Montana, Jr., grew up as a three-sport star at Ringgold High School. He could have gone into baseball, basketball, or football. Joe's dad pushed him toward football and a Notre Dame athletic scholarship. His mother, Teresa, was as determined that her son earn a degree as Joe's father was that he win a varsity letter. The Notre Dame scholarship gave the Montanas' son what both his parents wanted.

Joe Montana grew up in a typically middle-class family. They owned a modest house, took camping trips together, and asked their son only that he keep up his marks while developing into an athlete. If Joe Montana had never succeeded in professional sports, he would have been much like his father. He would be a good neighbor, married with a family and a routine job. Of course, as the best quarterback in the NFL during the 1980s, his job was far from routine. He lived a special life.

Most people work all year, with two weeks off for a vacation. The jobs of pro football players run from July, when they report for preseason camp, until the season ends late in December. However, since Joe has led his team into post-season play every year since the strike-shortened 1982 campaign, he works into January.

A typical "work week" for Joe Montana, when the NFL season is underway, starts on Monday morning. The previous day's game is over, and everyone is thinking about the next opponent. The first day the coaching staff and players watch videos of the team they are going to play. Joe starts to memorize about 100 plays that may be called on the coming Sunday. Through the week Joe watches films and tapes and studies "the play book." The coaches will also pick out about 20 plays to be used in the opening quarter. This will be "the script" and be followed unless something unusual happens that changes the way the game is going.

Joe does not actually scrimmage during the week. No one knocks him down with a bone-crunching sack. He practices the plays he might call, sharpening the instinct that tells him where to step to avoid onrushing defenders. Actually, this is the key to Joe Montana's success as a passer. No one has ever been better at making the quick decision to throw to the primary receiver or go to an alternate one. On a typical play, a wide receiver will run a deep pattern. Joe might wait until his man reaches the spot where the pass should be thrown. Or he might "read" the way the defense has reacted and abandon his primary target for a back making a delayed break into a cleared-out area. Or in the two or three seconds he has to decide, Joe might elect to simply flip the ball to a running back behind the line. When all his passing options are covered, Joe avoids an interception by ducking to the ground and escaping from the huge defensive linemen. Even so, injury cannot be avoided forever. Joe has had his share of them. Sometimes he has missed games and often he has played hurt. Of all the protective gear he must wear, Joe's flak jacket hinders him the most. It is a heavy leather vest he began to wear in 1982. A quarterback's ribs are vulnerable. The jacket is bulky, but Joe has adapted to it.

Joe had a good season in 1983 as the 49ers won 10 and lost 6 to win the Western Division title before losing to Washington in the championship playoffs by a field goal kicked with 40 seconds left to play. It was a bitter defeat because a number of calls by the officials seemed unfair. Joe Montana rarely complains about the officiating in the NFL. Over a season, the bad calls tend to balance out. However, when a title is on the line in a single game, then every call has to be right one.

When the 49ers reported for training camp in 1984, they were still angry about the way they had lost to Washington. They were more determined than ever to go to the Super Bowl. It was to be Joe's best season, with the team winning 15 games and losing only once. Joe led the league in most statistics while compiling his highest NFL quarterback rating, 102.9.

The team did not have to depend as much on Montana's

Like all quarterbacks, Joe is under constant threat from defensive linemen.

throwing. They now had two big backs, Wendell Tyler and Roger Craig. The dynamic San Francisco offensive line could now do more than set up a pocket to protect Joe. They could also blast holes in the defense for Tyler and Craig to drive through.

It took a last-second field goal by Ray Wersching to win the opener from Detroit, 30–27. Maybe the 49ers were guilty of looking ahead to the next game when they would have a chance for revenge against the Washington Redskins. The 49ers blew into the game, supercharged with emotion. They opened a 27–3 lead in the first quarter. By halftime they were emotionally drained and physically worn out. The second half was played on sheer guts. Washington piled up 28 points, but San Francisco managed to score 10 and win the game, 37–31.

In the next game Joe was hurt. His ribs were sore, and he could not finish against New Orleans, although the team won 30–20. The next week Matt Cavanaugh, Joe's backup, made his first start in two years and beat the Philadelphia Eagles, 21–9. Joe Montana got ready to play the next game against Atlanta.

The game was a low-scoring victory for San Francisco, 14–5. In a Monday night game against the New York Giants, the 49ers chalked up an easy 31–10 win, their sixth in a row. Still undefeated, they took on the Pittsburgh Steelers at Candlestick Park. Joe has always felt different about his "hometown" team. He grew up only 25 miles away from Pittsburgh in Monongahela. However, sentiment does not win or lose ball games. Joe has beaten the Steelers with great performances, but on October 14, 1984, he had a game he would like to forget. With the score tied, 17–17, and 2:03 left to play, Joe Montana was intercepted. The Steelers linebacker, Bryan Hinkle, grabbed the ball and rumbled 43 yards before being dragged down on the 3-yard line. From there it was just a chip-shot kick for Gary Anderson, the Pittsburgh field goal specialist to win the game, 20–17. It was the only game San Francisco would lose all season.

With the 49ers 6-1 and Miami 7-0, the fans and press began to anticipate a Super Bowl showdown between the two teams and their great quarterbacks. Dan Marino also came from the western part of Pennsylvania that grew superstar quarterbacks. However, before that could happen, San Francisco had to beat the Chicago Bears for the NFL Conference Championship.

Sacks like this one have left Montana with broken ribs and sore shoulders.

Chicago has long been known as the "Big Bad Bears." Going back to the early days of the NFL, when Bronko Nagurski and Red Grange played for owner-coach George Halas, the Bears have always had a hard-nosed attitude. In 1985 they were coached by Mike Ditka, himself a rugged ex-Bears linebacker. They had the great running back, Walter Payton, but nothing else beyond a strong defense. The Bears' quarterback, Jim McMahon, who could turn in sensational performances, was injured and not able to play. Although it was Chicago, the "Monsters of the Midway," who bragged

A sidelined Montana talks with his backup, Matt Cavanaugh.

Quarterbacks depend on a strong defense to give them time to find a receiver.

about their defense, the 49ers vowed to shut them out and show which team was the toughest.

In 17 games, the Bears had allowed only four teams to gain as much as 100 yards. Yet, from the opening kickoff, it was clear they could not contain the 49ers. San Francisco took a quick lead on a field goal. They added another three-pointer after Joe fumbled away a chance to score close to the Bears' goal line. It also became evident Chicago could go nowhere against the 49ers' charged-up defense. The game was not as close as the halftime score, 6–0, seemed. Joe hit for a touchdown early in the final period for a 13–0 lead, and another touchdown and field goal made the final score 23–0.

Miami had won their fifth straight American Football Conference title. It would be the Dolphins against the 49ers in the Super Bowl.

Chapter 5

Super Bowl XIX, following the 1984 season, matched the two top quarterbacks in the NFL. Dan Marino, leader of the Miami Dolphins, had thrown 55 touchdown passes in 18 games. This incredible number looked even more impressive against Joe Montana's below-par performance in the playoffs. Both teams had exceptional season records. San Francisco had lost only one game during the season. Miami came into the Super Bowl with a 16–2 record. Many football writers said that it was the tougher conference.

The 49ers would have one advantage. Although the Super Bowl is played on a neutral field, the NFL had made Stanford Stadium, located in Palo Alto, just outside San Francisco, the site for the game. Coach Walsh told his team they could live at home during the pregame practices.

San Francisco is one of America's most exciting cities to visit. Its charms, though, were too familiar to the 49er players to distract them. The Miami Dolphins, however, not only had to live in a hotel, separated from their families, but they were also out riding cable cars, strolling along Fisherman's Wharf, and taking in other tourist attractions. The 49ers were focused on the game.

Joe Montana was able to follow his usual routine when living at home. It did mean driving to San Jose, where the 49ers are headquartered, or to Candlestick Park for practices. However, it also meant evenings with Jennifer Wallace, his fiancée.

Super Bowl games get a tremendous buildup in the media.

Joe greets his San Francisco teammates before the game.

During the ten days leading up to the game to be played on January 20, 1985, reporters pestered Joe with questions. They wanted to make the game a confrontation between Joe and Dan Marino. Joe Montana would have none of it. He knew it was a game between teams. If he were egged into competing with Marino, it would throw the 49ers game plan out of synch.

Dan Marino's strength is throwing long passes, and Joe uses short ones. This is not a matter of different abilities, but of the way each team was put together by its coaches. Joe could throw deep, of course. However, it worked better if he relied on his hard-hitting backs, Wendell Tyler and Roger Craig, and mixed in short passes to keep the defense off balance.

Even so, the first time the 49ers had the ball in the Super Bowl game, Joe Montana threw deep. It did not work. He tried again. He was lucky he was not intercepted. As it was, San Francisco had to give the ball up to Miami, and they began a march up the field. The Dolphins used a no-huddle offense. Marino called the signals, and the plays were run off quickly. Miami moved 45 yards in 7 plays, and the drive ended with a 37-yard field goal by Uwe von Schamann.

The 49ers shifted to a nickel defense, so called because a fifth defensive back replaces a linebacker. It is more flexible and is the best setup against the hurry-up no-huddle tactics of Miami.

Joe Montana settled into the 49ers' style of play, and controlling the ball, San Francisco went 78 yards in 8 plays. Then Joe rolled out and hit Carl Monroe for a touchdown.

The Dolphins bounced back with a Marino pass to his tight end Dan Johnson. The touchdown covered only two yards, but long gainers had set up the score. Then, in the second quarter, the 49ers simply took over. They scored three touchdowns. Roger Craig was a terror, both at catching passes

Montana's short passes have often brought the 49ers back from near defeat.

and running the ball. He slanted in from 8 yards out for one touchdown. Joe, seeing the Dolphin secondary was following pass receivers downfield, began running the ball. Mixed in with short passes, the 49ers took a commanding 28–16 lead at the half.

The 49ers put the game out of reach in the third quarter by scoring twice. Ray Wersching kicked a field goal, and Joe Montana hit Roger Craig for a 16-yard touchdown pass. The final score was 38–16. Dan Marino completed 29 of 50 passes for 318 yards but was sacked four times. He was intercepted twice. Joe Montana threw for 331 yards and ran for 59. He was voted the MVP of the game but was happy for more than that. It had been a total team victory. The 49ers had played a perfect game. They had scored on five possessions in a row in the second and third quarters.

Joe's parents, along with many relatives and friends from back home, had been at the game. When he took his mother and father to the San Francisco airport the day after the game, Joe slipped the ring from his first Super Bowl game off his finger and gave it to his dad. There would be a new one for Joe to wear, and there should be more to come after that. Anyway, Joe was even more interested in the ring he would put on Jennifer Wallace's finger when they were married the next month. After two hasty marriages, it seemed Joe had found happiness at last.

Joe Montana was sitting on top of a football-shaped world. He was in the second year of a six-year contract that paid him $900,000 a season to play football. He had proposed to Jennifer by hiring a plane to tow a sign, "JEN WILL YOU MARRY ME?" Now married, they soon were building their present home in Redwood City. Their first baby, Alexandra, was on the way when the new 1985 season began to crumble.

No one knows why Joe Montana was singled out for

insinuations that his below-par performance in the early season was due to a drug problem. It is a price celebrities seem to have to pay even when the rumors are false and malicious. Joe played despite a flu bug, his infant daughter also caught the flu and had to be rushed to a hospital. It was the low point of a season that might yet be salvaged. Despite their record, the 49ers could qualify for a Wild Card spot in the playoffs if they beat the New York Giants. However, they lost 17–3 after Joe injured his shoulder on a blind-side hit by Lawrence Taylor. Bad as the season had been, things got worse in 1986.

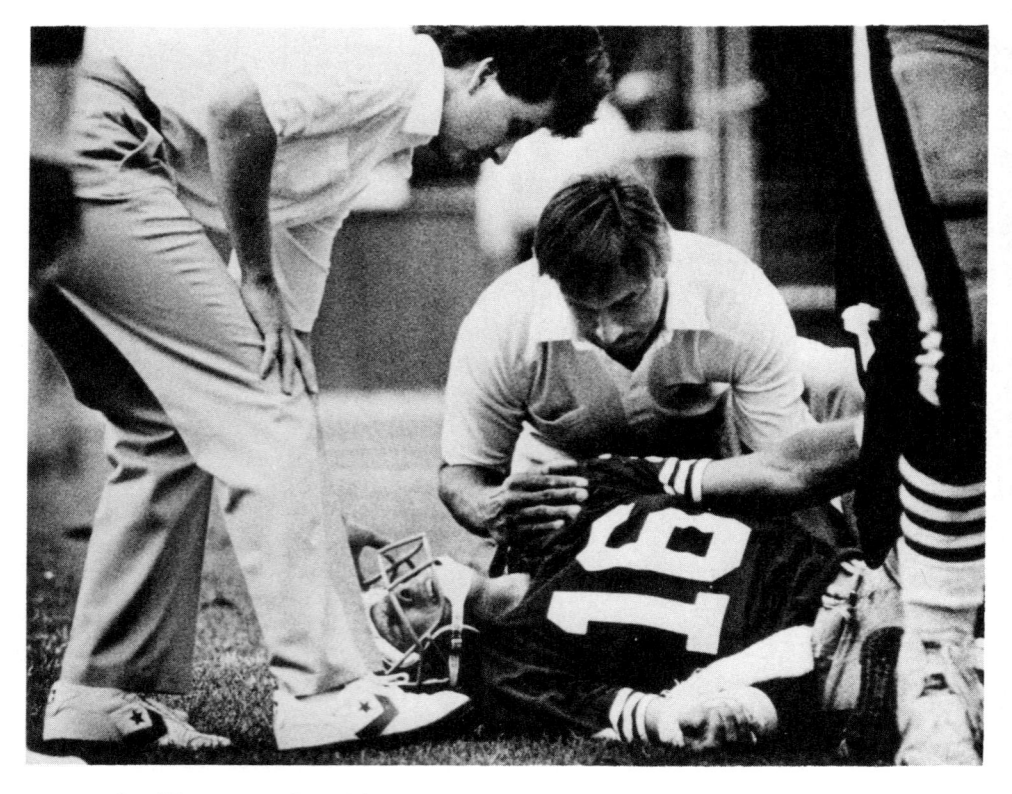

Joe did not get up from this sack. The coaching staff looks at his injured shoulder.

An NFL quarterback learns to play in pain. Joe Montana was far from being an exception. He had knee surgery back in 1982, but his real problem was a sciatic nerve condition in his back. Then, in the season's opening game at Tampa Bay, Montana threw out his back after releasing the ball in an awkward position. He was carried from the field, and an examination showed a ruptured disk. The doctors also found a congenital narrowing of the spinal column. Even if an operation made it possible to play again, the doctors told Joe it would be foolish to ever try again.

The day after the surgery, Joe began working with weights. When his teammates, Ronnie Lott, Dwight Clark, and Wendell Tyler visited his hospital room, they found him sitting up and gingerly hefting small lead weights. He wanted to rejoin his team as soon as he could. Amazingly, Joe made it back before the season was over. He had missed eight games, but his replacement, Steve Young, had filled in adequately. The 49ers were 5 and 3 and still in the running for a playoff spot. Joe led the way to five more victories in the last seven games, and San Francisco won the Western Division championship.

Then the bubble burst. Playing their nemesis, the New York Giants, at the home field of the Eastern Division champions, they were wiped out 49–3. Montana was knocked out of the game in the second quarter. He went down under a hard charge by noseguard Jim Burt, but his back held up.

In 1987 Joe threw more touchdown passes than ever before. He brought his team into the NFC playoff round. This time Minnesota drubbed the 49ers 36–24 in a game more one-sided than the score indicated. In the third quarter, Joe Montana was replaced by Steve Young. Was it the end for Joe Montana? He was nearly thirty-two, and his replacement was only twenty-six.

As Joe Montana continued to struggle with injuries, Steve Young (#8) began to step in more and more.

In 1988 Joe had a difficult time in preseason training. He was slowed by nagging injuries. There were old ones, like his gimpy knee, and a new one to his elbow. His ribs were tender as usual, and his back was a time bomb ready to explode. Steve Young opened the 1988 season, and Joe did not start until the fourth game. Even then, Coach Walsh was quick to pull Joe out of a game and substitute Young at quarterback.

Despite the constant switching of quarterbacks, San Francisco won another Western Division title with a 10–6 record. Coach Walsh finally let his veteran quarterback take charge. First came revenge against Minnesota. The Vikings had knocked the 49ers out of the playoffs the year before. They had stopped Montana, who now had not thrown a touchdown pass in three years of post-season play.

It was different this year when the teams met on New Year's Day in Candlestick Park. Joe hit three TDs, all to Jerry Rice, and the 49ers won 34–9. They were on their way to the NFC title game with the Chicago Bears. Once more Joe threw three touchdown passes, had no interceptions, and completed 17 passes for 288 yards as the 49ers blew out the Bears in Chicago, 28–3. The victory meant a return to the Super Bowl for Joe Montana and the 49ers.

Chapter 6

Joe Montana's first visit to the Super Bowl, when the 49ers beat the Cincinnati Bengals 26–21 in 1982, had been made possible when he beat the Dallas Cowboys with the pass to Dwight Clark that was known as "The Catch." Seven years later, Joe would pull out of thin air another Super Bowl victory over the Bengals with what is remembered as "The Drive."

Boomer Esiason, a blond lefthanded thrower, was the top-rated passer in the NFL. Because of injuries that kept him mostly idle until the final month of the season, Montana's stats were below his average. However, put Joe in a Super Bowl, and he will rise to the heights.

For the first half, the defense of both teams dominated. Each team had been held to a field goal. Then, at the start of the third quarter, the Bengals took charge. They gained on the ground, and Boomer hit on 23-yard and 11-yard passes. Cincinnati controlled the ball for almost ten minutes before taking the lead on another field goal, 6–3. The 49ers evened the score with their own field goal. Then, just before the fourth quarter began, Stanford Jennings took the kickoff straight up the field for a 93-yard touchdown run. The Bengals led 13–6 and still neither team had scored on a pass or play from scrimmage.

Suddenly Joe Montana began to click. After he hooked up with Jerry Rice for a 30-yard gainer, the fourth quarter began with a perfect 40-yard fly pattern pass to Roger Craig. After a near interception at the Bengals' goal line, Joe found Rice at the 5, and the wide receiver swung into the end zone. The conversion tied the game 13–13.

Back came Boomer, mixing passes with running plays, until a field goal was kicked for a 16–13 lead with the clock

Joe Montana gives directions and encouragement from the sidelines to his backup quarterback.

running out. A penalty on the kickoff moved the 49ers back to their 8-yard line. There was 3:10 left. Down on the field, Joe Montana remembered the Dallas game in 1982. Up in the stands his mother, Teresa, said she thought of the 1979 Cotton Bowl when Joe had brought the Fighting Irish from behind to beat Texas.

Today's finish would be yet another miracle worked by Joe Montana. It lives in football lore as "The Drive." It required 11 plays: Montana to Craig, 8 yards; Montana to Frank, 7 yards; Montana to Rice, 7 yards; a Craig run for one yard. Then came the two-minute warning. When play resumed, it was a Craig run for 4 yards, followed by a San Francisco time-out, then Montana to Rice, 17 yards; Montana to Craig, 13 yards; Montana pass incomplete; Montana to Craig, 4 yards, but an ineligible receiver downfield cost a 10-yard penalty. The ball was on the Cincinnati 45, second down, 20 yards to go. Montana to Rice, 27 yards; Montana to Craig, 8 yards; San Francisco time-out. Ball on the Cincinnati 10, second down. Montana to Taylor, 10 yards . . . Touchdown! The extra point was kicked, and the 49ers led 20–16 with 0:24 left. Time ran out, and the San Francisco 49ers were Super Bowl champions for the third time in Joe Montana's reign.

The Most Valuable Player award went to wide receiver, Jerry Rice. He said Joe Montana should have had it, but Joe wasn't selfish. He already had two Super Bowl MVP trophies. Anyway, there might be another chance. The 49ers were the best team in the NFL, and Joe was at his peak as a quarterback.

The "Passer of the Eighties" ended the decade ranked as the top passer in NFL history. Joe Montana had a rating of 94.0 over 11 seasons. This rating compares the passer's completion percentage, average gain, touchdown and

Pleased, Joe Montana and Jerry Rice congratulate each other after a touchdown pass to Rice.

interception percentage to a standard. Among the former star NFL quarterbacks, Roger Staubach was closest. He had left behind an 83.4 average for 11 seasons with Dallas.

The San Francisco 49ers won another Western Division title in 1989 with a 14–2–0 record. It was their fourth in a row. They had won eight of their division's last nine championships. They seemed to get better every passing season. There was a new coach. George Seifert, the defensive coach, took over when Walsh retired. The 49ers appeared to be even better balanced under Coach Seifert. As they powered their way toward another Super Bowl, people wondered how good they really might be. Minnesota, winner of the Central Division, was wiped out 41–13 and the Los Angeles Rams demolished 30–3. The 49ers seemed untested. Joe Montana moved the team with sharp passing, and the ball carriers chewed up long gains. It might take the Super Bowl to find out how good San Francisco really was.

The Denver Broncos, led by their great quarterback John Elway were back to try again to win the Super Bowl. This was their third try in the last four years. The Broncos practiced stopping Joe Montana's typical short passes. Their own quarterback, Elway, had one of the strongest arms in the history of the game.

Super Bowl XXIV was played January 28, 1990, at the Louisiana Superdome in New Orleans. The 49ers were 12-point favorites and lost no time proving the experts were right. The Denver defense had not given up more than 28 points in a game all season. San Francisco scored 27 by halftime. They scored constantly and evenly. Except for a missed conversion after the second touchdown in the first quarter, they would have registered exactly 14 points in each quarter. They led all the way in a relentless attack. The defense was magnificent. Denver managed an early field goal and one

Usually calm, cool, and collected, Montana saves his emotions for celebration.

meager touchdown on a John Elway 3-yard run. The final score was 55–10, the most devastating rout in the history of the Super Bowl.

Joe Montana? The quarterback who could only throw short passes? He threw for four touchdowns. The scoring passes went 20, 38, 28, and 35 yards. The game was a personal triumph for Joe Montana. He was named the Most Valuable Player, becoming the first to win this honor three times. It was his fourth Super Bowl, and Joe improved on his many records. He had yet to be intercepted after 122 passes in four Super Bowls. He had now completed 68 percent of all attempts for 11 touchdowns. In drubbing Denver, he had hit on 22 of 29 passes for 297 yards and a Super Bowl record of five touchdowns.

Joe Montana was elated by his team's performance. Although he plays with an icy calm, he does not hide his happiness when he and his teammates pull off a perfect play at a dramatic point in the game. Watch Joe and you will see him throw his arms overhead, helping the officials signal a touchdown call. Then he goes into a little jig of happiness.

Long after the locker rooms had emptied and the players had gone to the official 49ers victory party, Joe and Jennifer Montana were having their own family and friends celebration in their suite. Joe's parents, who now live in the San Francisco Bay area, were there. They are grandparents now of Joe and Jennifer's three children. Alexandra has a year-younger sister, Elizabeth, and a brother Nathaniel who was not yet a year old when his father threw the five TDs against Denver.

Other relatives from back in Monongahela, Pennsylvania, and close friends who had grown up with Joe or were part of his new life in California shared in Joe Montana's happiness. Joe shares himself with the public as much as is possible. However, he is primarily a private person who chooses his friends carefully. He was thirty-three years old when he won his fourth Super Bowl game. Although he will play as long as he can avoid a career-ending injury or a loss of ability due to age, Joe Montana is looking to the future. He would like to coach but knows that such a job would continue to keep him apart from his family.

He has studied the wine business and the vineyards of California near where he lives. Joe is also learning the food preparation part of the restaurant business. Whatever Joe does after he hangs up his jersey with its famous No. 16, he will have prepared for it as thoroughly as he has readied himself for his extraordinary football career. Meanwhile, the San

Despite his injuries, Joe Montana continues to lead his team season after season.

Francisco 49ers moved into the 1990s on the still wonderful arm of Joe Montana.

The 1990 season seemed to be played by the rest of the league as though the San Francisco 49ers and Joe Montana were destined to make another appearance in the Super Bowl. It was taken for granted that Joe would extend the dynasty for another year. Once more the 49ers won the Western Division title and had the home-field advantage for the playoff game for the National Conference championship. Beat the tough New York Giants, and they would head for Tampa, Florida, and Super Bowl XXV. They never got there.

San Francisco had been shocked a year earlier when a big earthquake had hit the Bay area. Thousands of people had been at Candlestick Park for the World Series when the earth began to move. On January 20, 1991, it was a football crowd that was shocked. Maybe Joe Montana had pulled off so many last-ditch victories that the public took his miracles for granted. But it was the Giants placekicker, Matt Bahr, whose 42-yard field goal with no time remaining tumbled San Francisco out of its expected Super Bowl appearance. It was Bahr's fifth field goal. He had provided all the Giants scoring in an upset 15–13 victory.

Joe Montana would not have been able to rally the 49ers even if any time had been left. He had been knocked out of the game in the fourth quarter when he had been sacked. Dazed, Joe was seated on the bench, hoping his teammates could hang on to the narrow lead he had left them. Yet even if they had gone on to Super Bowl XXV, Joe Montana would not have been able to pass his way to more records. When Joe was examined after the game, it was discovered that his right hand had been broken. It would never have healed in a week's time.

In 1991, Montana was sidelined with a torn tendon in his

throwing arm and missed the entire season. For the 1992 season, while his arm was still healing, Montana only played in one game. By the end of the season, Montana's backup quarterback, Steve Young, had earned the starting position. Although Montana was ready to play in 1993, head coach George Siefert announced that the starting quarterback would be Young.

Montana began to shop around for another team that would put him in the starting line-up. When Montana began receiving offers from other teams, the 49ers offered Montana his job back again. But by then it was too late. Montana signed a 3-year, $10 million contract with the Kansas City Chiefs.

After being out of play for two seasons, Montana made a phenomenal comeback as a Kansas City Chief. In 1993, he passed for 2,144 yards, as the Chiefs ended the regular season at 11–5. Montana led the Chiefs all the way to the AFC championship game. In the title game, Montana suffered a concussion, and the Buffalo Bills denied the Chiefs their first trip to the Super Bowl in over twenty years.

Montana had another successful season in 1994. The Chiefs were eliminated from playoff contention by veteran quarterback Dan Marino and the Miami Dolphins. After a grueling wild-card game, the Dolphins defeated the Chiefs 27–17.

The 1990s marked the final decade for Joe Montana, the "Passer of the Eighties." Joe announced his retirement on April 18, 1995, and on December 15, 1997, the 49ers retired his number. Football is a team sport, and it takes a championship season for everyone to get to the Super Bowl. The NFL is a tough world where it is very hard to repeat success. Joe Montana kept trying, and no one ever tried harder than the "Comeback Kid."

Career Statistics

YEAR	CLUB	PASS ATT.	PASS COMPL.	PASS YARDS	TOUCH-DOWNS	INTER-CEPTS
1979	San Francisco	23	13	96	1	0
1980	San Francisco	273	176	1795	15	9
1981	San Francisco	488	311	3565	19	12
1982	San Francisco	346	213	2613	17	11
1983	San Francisco	515	332	3910	26	12
1984	San Francisco	432	279	3630	28	10
1985	San Francisco	494	303	3653	27	13
1986	San Francisco	307	191	2236	8	9
1987	San Francisco	398	266	3054	31	13
1988	San Francisco	397	238	2981	18	10
1989	San Francisco	386	271	3521	26	8
1990	San Francisco	520	321	3944	26	16
1991	San Francisco			INJURED		
1992	San Francisco	21	15	126	2	0
1993	Kansas City	298	181	2144	13	7
1994	Kansas City	493	299	3283	16	9
	TOTAL	5391	3409	40,551	273	139

Index

A
Air Force Academy, 10
Anderson, Gary, 38
Anderson, Kenny, 28
Atlanta Falcons, 37

B
Bahr, Matt, 60
Bradshaw, Terry, 18
Browner, Jim, 9
Browner, Ross, 28, 30
Burgmeier, Ted, 10
Burt, Jim, 49
Buth, Doug, 9

C
Campbell, Earl, 12
Candlestick Park, 24, 37, 44, 51, 60
Cavanaugh, Matt, 37, 39
Chicago Bears, 38–39, 41, 51
Cincinnati Bengals, 28, 52–54
Clark, Dwight, 19, 21, 23, 26, 49, 52
Clemson University, 19
Conley, Russ, 10
Cotton Bowl, 11, 12, 13
Craig, Roger, 37, 45, 47, 53, 54

D
Dallas, Cowboys, 24, 26, 52
DeBerg, Steven, 18, 20, 23
Denver Broncos, 23, 56, 58
Detroit Lions, 28, 37
Devine, Dan, 9, 10, 15, 30
Ditka, Mike, 39

E
Elway, John, 56, 58
Esiason, Boomer, 52, 53–54

F
Ferguson, Vegas, 12, 13

H
Haines, Kris, 13, 14–15
Heavans, Jerome, 12
Hinkle, Bryan, 37
Hodge, David, 14
Hunter, Al, 9

J
Jennings, Stanford, 53
Johnson, Dan, 45
Jones, Ed ("Too Tall"), 26

K
Kelly, Jim, 17
Koegel, Tim, 13

L
Los Angeles Rams, 56
Lott, Ronnie, 24, 49

M
MacAfee, Ken, 11
McLane, Mark, 9

McMahon, Jim, 39
Marino, Dan, 17, 38, 43, 45, 47
Miami Dolphins, 38, 41, 43–45, 47
Minnesota Vikings, 51
Mitchell, David, 11
Monroe, Larry, 33
Montana, Joseph Sr., 33–34, 47
Montana, Teresa, 33, 34, 47, 54
Moses, Kim, 10

N
New Orleans Saints, 21
New York Giants, 24, 37, 48, 49, 60
Northwestern University, 9

O
Oakland Raiders, 30

P
Payton, Walter, 39
Philadelphia Eagles, 37
Pittsburgh Steelers, 18, 37–38
Plunkett, Jim, 30
Purdue University, 10

R
Rice, Jerry, 53, 54
Ringgold High School, 34

S
San Francisco 49ers, 5, 17, 18–20, 23–24, 26, 28, 30–31, 35–39, 41, 43–45, 47, 48, 49, 51, 52–54, 56, 58, 59–61
Seifert, George, 56
Shearer, Brad, 12

Simpson, O.J., 18–19
Solomon, Freddie, 26
Staubach, Roger, 56
Stuckey, Jim, 26
Super Bowl XVI, 26, 28, 30
Super Bowl XIX, 43
Super Bowl XXIV, 56, 58
Super Bowl XXV, 60

T
Tampa Bay Buccaneers, 24
Taylor, Lawrence, 48
Tyler, Wendell, 37, 45, 49

U
Unis, Joe, 15
University of Houston, 13–15
University of North Carolina, 9
University of Notre Dame, 7, 9–15, 17, 34
University of Pittsburgh, 12
University of Southern California, 12
University of Tennessee, 12
University of Texas, 11, 12

V
von Schamann, Uwe, 45

W
Wallace, Jennifer, 44, 47, 58
Walsh, Bill, 18, 19, 20–21, 23, 26, 28, 51, 56
Washington Redskins, 35, 36, 37
Wersching, Ray, 26, 28, 37, 47
White, Danny, 26

Y
Young, Steve, 49, 51

Locust Grove Elementary
31230 Constitution Hwy
Locust Grove, VA 22508

3567

②

RL-6.4